Ralph Waldo Emerson

Fortune of the Republic

Lecture Delivered at the Old South Church, March 30, 1878

Ralph Waldo Emerson

Fortune of the Republic
Lecture Delivered at the Old South Church, March 30, 1878

ISBN/EAN: 9783337005115

Printed in Europe, USA, Canada, Australia, Japan

Cover: Foto ©ninafisch / pixelio.de

More available books at **www.hansebooks.com**

FORTUNE OF THE REPUBLIC.

LECTURE

DELIVERED AT THE OLD SOUTH CHURCH,

March 30, 1878.

BY

RALPH WALDO EMERSON.

BOSTON:

HOUGHTON, OSGOOD AND COMPANY.

The Riverside Press, Cambridge.

1879.

FORTUNE OF THE REPUBLIC.

———◆———

IT is a rule that holds in economy as well as in hydraulics, that you must have a source higher than your tap. The mills, the shops, the theatre and the caucus, the college and the church, have all found out this secret. The sailors sail by chronometers that do not lose two or three seconds in a year, ever since Newton explained to Parliament that the way to improve navigation was to get good watches, and to offer public premiums for a better time-keeper than any then in use. The manufacturers rely on turbines of hydraulic perfection; the carpet-mill, on mordants and dyes which exhaust the skill of the chemist; the calico print, on designers

1

of genius who draw the wages of artists, not
of artisans. Wedgewood, the eminent pot-
ter, bravely took the sculptor Flaxman to
counsel, who said, " Send to Italy, search the
museums for the forms of old Etruscan vases,
urns, water-pots, domestic and sacrificial ves-
sels of all kinds." They built great works and
called their manufacturing village Etruria.
Flaxman, with his Greek taste, selected and
combined the loveliest forms, which were
executed in English clay; sent boxes of these
as gifts to every court of Europe, and formed
the taste of the world. It was a renaissance
of the breakfast table and china-closet. The
brave manufacturers made their fortune. The
jewellers imitated the revived models in sil-
ver and gold.

The theatre avails itself of the best talent
of poet, of painter, and of amateur of taste, to
make the *ensemble* of dramatic effect. The
marine insurance office has its mathematical
counsellor to settle averages; the life-assur-

ance, its table of annuities. The wine merchant has his analyst and taster, the more exquisite the better. He has also, I fear, his debts to the chemist as well as to the vineyard.

(*x*) Our modern wealth stands on a few staples, and the interest nations took in our war was exasperated by the importance of the cotton trade. And what is cotton? One plant out of some two hundred thousand known to the botanist, vastly the larger part of which are reckoned weeds. And what is a weed? A plant whose virtues have not yet been discovered, — every one of the two hundred thousand probably yet to be of utility in the arts. As Bacchus of the vine, Ceres of the wheat, as Arkwright and Whitney were the demi-gods of cotton, so prolific Time will yet bring an inventor to every plant. There is not a property in nature but a mind is born to seek and find it. For it is not the plants or the animals, innumerable as they are, nor

the whole magazine of material nature that
can give the sum of power, but the infinite
applicability of these things in the hands of
thinking man, every new application being
equivalent to a new material.

Our sleepy civilization, ever since Roger
Bacon and Monk Schwartz invented gun-
powder, has built its whole art of war, all
fortification by land and sea, all drill and
military education, on that one compound, —
all is an extension of a gun-barrel, — and is
very scornful about bows and arrows, and
reckons Greeks and Romans and Middle
Ages little better than Indians and bow-and-
arrow times. As if the earth, water, gases,
lightning and caloric had not a million ener-
gies, the discovery of any one of which could
change the art of war again, and put an end
to war by the exterminating forces man can
apply.

Now, if this is true in all the useful and
in the fine arts, that the direction must be

drawn from a superior source or there will be no good work, does it hold less in our social and civil life?

In our popular politics you may note that each aspirant who rises above the crowd, however at first making his obedient apprenticeship in party tactics, if he have sagacity, soon learns that it is by no means by obeying the vulgar weathercock of his party, the resentments, the fears, and whims of it, that real power is gained, but that he must often face and resist the party, and abide by his resistance, and put them in fear; that the only title to their permanent respect, and to a larger following, is to see for himself what is the real public interest, and to stand for that; — that is a principle, and all the cheering and hissing of the crowd must by and by accommodate itself to it. Our times easily afford you very good examples.

The law of water and all fluids is true of wit. Prince Metternich said, " Revolutions begin in the best heads and run steadily down to the populace." It is a very old observation; not truer because Metternich said it, and not less true.

There have been revolutions which were not in the interest of feudalism and barbarism, but in that of society. And these are distinguished not by the numbers of the combatants nor the numbers of the slain, but by the motive. . No interest now attaches to the wars of York and Lancaster, to the wars of German, French, and Spanish emperors, which were only dynastic wars, but to those in which a principle was involved. These are read with passionate interest and never lose their pathos by time. When the cannon is aimed by ideas, when men with religious convictions are behind it, when men die for what they live for, and the mainspring that works daily urges them to hazard all, then the cannon articulates its explosions with the voice of a man, then the rifle seconds the cannon and the fowling-piece the rifle, and the women make the cartridges, and all shoot at one mark; then gods join in the combat; then poets are born, and the better code of laws at last records the victory.

Now the culmination of these triumphs of humanity — and which did virtually include the extinction of slavery — is the planting of America.

At every moment some one country more than any other represents the sentiment and the future of mankind. None will doubt that America occupies this place in the opinion of nations, as is proved by the fact of the vast immigration into this country from all the nations of Western and Central Europe. And when the adventurers have planted themselves and looked about, they send back all the money they can spare to bring their friends.

Meantime they find this country just passing through a great crisis in its history, as necessary as lactation or dentition or puberty to the human individual. We are in these days settling for ourselves and our descendants questions which, as they shall be determined in one way or the other, will make the peace and prosperity or the calamity of the next ages. The questions of Education, of Society, of Labor, the direction of talent, of character, the nature and habits of the American, may well occupy us, and more the question of Religion.

The new conditions of mankind in America are really favorable to progress, the removal of absurd restrictions and antique inequalities. The mind is always better the more it is used, and here it is kept in practice. The humblest is daily challenged to give his opinion on practical questions, and while civil and social freedom exists, nonsense even has a favorable effect. Cant is good to provoke common sense. The Catholic Church, tho trance-mediums, the rebel paradoxes, exasperate the common sense. The wilder the paradox, the more sure is Punch to put it in the pillory.

The lodging the power in the people, as in republican forms, has the effect of holding things closer to common sense; for a court or an aristocracy, which must always be a small minority, can more easily run into follies than a republic, which has too many observers, — each with a vote in his hand, — to allow its head to be turned by any kind of nonsense: since hunger, thirst, cold, the cries of children, and debt, are always holding the masses hard to the essential duties.

One hundred years ago the American people attempted to carry out the bill of political rights to an almost ideal perfection. They have made great strides in that direction since. They are now proceeding, instructed by their success, and by their many failures, to carry out not the bill of rights, but the bill of human duties.

And look what revolution that attempt involves. Hitherto government has been that of the single person or of the aristocracy. In this country the attempt to resist these elements, it is asserted, must throw us into the government not quite of mobs, but in practice of an inferior class of professional politicians, who by means of newspapers and caucuses really thrust their unworthy minority into the place of the old aristocracy on the one side, and of the good, industrious, well-taught but unambitious population on the other, win the posts of power, and give their direction to affairs. Hence liberal congresses and legislatures ordain, to the surprise of the people, equivocal, interested, and vicious measures. The men themselves are suspected and charged with lobbying and being lobbied. No measure is attempted for itself, but the opinion of the people is courted in the first place, and the measures are perfunctorily carried through as secondary. We do not choose our own candidate, no, nor any other man's first choice, — but only the available candidate, whom, perhaps, no man loves. We do not speak what we think, but grope after the practicable and available. Instead of character, there is a studious exclusion of character. The people are feared and flattered. They are not reprimanded. The country is governed in bar-rooms, and in the mind of bar-rooms. The low can best win the low, and each aspirant for power vies with his rival which can stoop lowest, and depart widest from himself.

The partisan on moral, even on religious questions, will choose a proven rogue who can answer the tests, over an honest, affectionate, noble gentleman; the partisan ceasing to be a man that he may be a sectarian.

The spirit of our political economy is low and degrading. The precious metals are not so precious as they are esteemed. Man exists for his own sake, and not to add a laborer to the state. The spirit of our political action, for the most part, considers nothing less than the sacredness of man. Party sacrifices man to the measure.

We have seen the great party of property and education in the country drivelling and huckstering away, for views of party fear or advantage, every principle of humanity and the dearest hopes of mankind; the trustees of power only energetic when mischief could be done, imbecile as corpses when evil was to be prevented.

Our great men succumb so far to the forms of the day as to peril their integrity for the sake of adding to the weight of their personal character the authority of office, or making a real government titular. Our politics are full of adventurers, who having by education and social innocence a good repute in the state, break away from the law of honesty and think they can afford to join the devil's party. 'T is odious, these offenders in high life. You rally to the support of old charities and the cause of literature, and there, to be sure, are these brazen faces. In this innocence you are puzzled how to meet them; must shake hands with them, under protest. We feel toward them as the minister about the Cape Cod farm, — in the old time when the minister was still invited, in the spring, to make a prayer for the blessing of a piece of land, — the good pastor being brought to the spot, stopped short: " No, this land does not want a prayer, this land wants manure."

> " 'T is virtue which they want, and wanting it,
> Honor no garment to their backs can fit."

Parties keep the old names, but exhibit a surprising fugacity in creeping out of one snake-skin into another of equal ignominy and lubricity, and the grasshopper on the turret of Faneuil Hall gives a proper hint of the men below.

Everything yields. The very glaciers are

viscous or regelate into conformity, and the
stiffest patriots falter and compromise; so
that *will* cannot be depended on to save us.

How rare are acts of will! We are all
living according to custom; we do as other
people do, and shrink from an act of our own.
Every such act makes a man famous, and we
can all count the few cases, — half a dozen in
our time, — when a public man ventured to
act as he thought, without waiting for orders
or for public opinion. John Quincy Adams
was a man of an audacious independence that
always kept the public curiosity alive in re-
gard to what he might do. None could pre-
dict his word, and a whole congress could
not gainsay it when it was spoken. General
Jackson was a man of will, and his phrase
on one memorable occasion, " I will take the
responsibility," is a proverb ever since.

The American marches with a careless
swagger to the height of power, very heed-
less of his own liberty, or of other peoples',

in his reckless confidence that he can have
all he wants, risking all the prized charters
of the human race, bought with battles and
revolutions and religion, gambling them all
away for a paltry selfish gain.

He sits secure in the possession of his vast
domain, rich beyond all experience in re-
sources, sees its inevitable force unlocking itself in elemental order day by day, year by
year; looks from his coal-fields, his wheat-
bearing prairie, his gold-mines, to his two
oceans on either side, and feels the security
that there can be no famine in a country
reaching through so many latitudes, no want
that cannot be supplied, no danger from any
excess of importation of art or learning into
a country of such native strength, such immense digestive power.

In proportion to the personal ability of
each man, he feels the invitation and career
which the country opens to him. He is easily
fed with wheat and game, with Ohio wine, but

his brain is also pampered by finer draughts, by political power and by the power in the railroad board, in the mills, or the banks. This elevates his spirits and gives, of course, an easy self-reliance that makes him self-willed and unscrupulous.

I think this levity is a reaction on the people from the extraordinary advantages and invitations of their condition. When we are most disturbed by their rash and immoral voting, it is not malignity, but recklessness. They are careless of politics, because they do not entertain the possibility of being seriously caught in meshes of legislation. They feel strong and irresistible. They believe that what they have enacted they can repeal if they do not like it. But one may run a risk once too often. They stay away from the polls, saying that one vote can do no good! Or they take another step, and say one vote can do no harm! and vote for something which they do not approve, because their party or set votes for it. Of course this puts them in the power of any party having a steady interest to promote, which does not conflict manifestly with the pecuniary interest of the voters. But if they should come to be interested in themselves and in their career, they would no more stay away from the election than from their own counting-room or the house of their friend.

The people are right-minded enough on ethical questions, but they must pay their debts, and must have the means of living well, and not pinching. So it is useless to rely on them to go to a meeting, or to give a vote, if any check from this must-have-the-money side arises. If a customer looks grave at their newspaper, or damns their member of Congress, they take another newspaper, and vote for another man. They must have money, for a certain style of living fast becomes necessary; they must take wine at the hotel, first, for the look of it, and second, for the purpose of sending the bottle to two or three gentlemen at the table; and presently, because they have got the taste, and do not feel that they have dined without it.

⁌ The record of the election now and then alarms people by the all but unanimous choice of a rogue and brawler. But how was it done? What lawless mob burst into the polls and threw in these hundreds of ballots in defiance of the magistrates? This was done by the very men you know, — the mildest, most sensible, best-natured people. The only account of this is, that they have been scared or warped into some association in their mind of the candidate with the interest of their trade or of their property.

⁌ Whilst each cabal urges its candidate, and at last brings, with cheers and street-demonstrations, men whose names are a knell to all hope of progress, the good and wise are hidden in their active retirements, and are quite out of question.

' These we must join to wake, for these are of the strain
That justice dare defend, and will the age maintain."

Yet we know, all over this country, men of
integrity, capable of action and of affairs,
with the deepest sympathy in all that con-
:erns the public, mortified by the national
disgrace, and quite capable of any sacrifice
except of their honor.

Faults in the working appear in our system,
as in all, but they suggest their own rem-
edies. After every practical mistake, out of
which any disaster grows, the people wake
and correct it with energy. And any dis-
turbances in politics, in civil or foreign wars,
sober them, and instantly show more virtue
and conviction in the popular vote. In each
new threat of faction the ballot has been,
beyond expectation, right and decisive.

'T is ever an inspiration, God only knows
whence; a sudden, undated perception of
eternal right coming into and correcting

things that were wrong; a perception that passes through thousands as readily as through one.

The gracious lesson taught by science to this country is, that the history of nature from first to last is incessant advance from less to more, from rude to finer organization, the globe of matter thus conspiring with the principle of undying hope in man. Nature works in immense time, and spends individuals and races prodigally to prepare new individuals and races. The lower kinds are one after one extinguished; the higher forms come in. The history of civilization, or the refining of certain races to wonderful power of performance, is analogous; but the best civilization yet is only valuable as a ground of hope.

Ours is the country of poor men. Here is practical democracy; here is the human race poured out over the continent to do itself justice; all mankind in its shirt-sleeves; not

grimacing like poor rich men in cities, pre-
tending to be rich, but unmistakably taking
off its coat to hard work, when labor is sure
to pay. This through all the country. For
really, though you see wealth in the capitals,
it is only a sprinkling of rich men in the
cities and at sparse points; the bulk of the
population is poor. In Maine, nearly every
man is a lumberer. In Massachusetts, every
twelfth man is a shoemaker, and the rest,
millers, farmers, sailors, fishermen.

Well, the result is, instead of the doleful
experience of the European economist, who
tells us, " In almost all countries the condition of the great body of the people is poor
and miserable," here that same great body
has arrived at a sloven plenty, — ham and
corn-cakes, tight roof, and coals enough have
been attained; an unbuttoned comfort, not
clean, not thoughtful, far from polished, without dignity in his repose; the man awkward
and restless if he have not something to do,

but honest and kind, for the most part, understanding his own rights and stiff to maintain them, and disposed to give his children a better education than he received.

The steady improvement of the public schools in the cities and the country enables the farmer or laborer to secure a precious primary education. It is rare to find a born American who cannot read and write. The facility with which clubs are formed by young men for discussion of social, political, and intellectual topics secures the notoriety of the questions.

Our institutions, of which the town is the unit, are all educational, for responsibility educates fast. The town meeting is, after the high school, a higher school. The legislature, to which every good farmer goes once on trial, is a superior academy.

The result appears in the power of invention, the freedom of thinking, in the readiness for reforms, eagerness for novelty, even for all the follies of false science; in the antipathy to secret societies, in the predominance of the Democratic party in the politics of the Union, and in the voice of the public even when irregular and vicious, — the voice of mobs, the voice of lynch law, — because it is thought to be, on the whole, the verdict, though badly spoken, of the greatest number.

All this forwardness and self-reliance cover self-government; proceed on the belief that as the people have made a government they can make another; that their union and law are not in their memory, but in their blood and condition. If they unmake a law, they can easily make a new one. In Mr. Webster's imagination the American Union was a huge Prince Rupert's drop, which will snap into atoms, if so much as the smallest end be shivered off. Now the fact is quite different from this. The people are loyal, law-abiding. They prefer order, and have no taste for misrule and uproar.

America was opened ,after the feudal mischief was spent, and so the people made a
good start. We began well. No inquisi-
tion here, no kings, no nobles, no dominant
church. Here heresy has lost its terrors.
We have eight or ten religions in every
large town, and the most that comes of it
is a degree or two on the thermometer of
fashion ; a pew in a particular church gives
an easier entrance to the subscription ball.
We began with freedom, and are defended
from shocks now for a century by the facility
with which through popular assemblies every
necessary measure of reform can instantly be
carried. A congress is a standing insurrec-
tion, and escapes the violence of accumulated
grievance. As the globe keeps its identity
by perpetual change, so our civil system, by
perpetual appeal to the people and accept-
ance of its reforms.

The government is acquainted with the
opinions of all classes, knows the leading

men in the middle class, knows the leaders of the humblest class. The President comes near enough to these; if he does not, the caucus does, — the primary ward and town meeting, and what is important does reach him.

The men, the women, all over this land shrill their exclamations of impatience and indignation at what is short-coming or is unbecoming in the government, — at the want of humanity, of morality, — ever on broad grounds of general justice, and not on the class-feeling which narrows the perception of English, French, German people at home. In this fact, that we are a nation of individuals, that we have a highly intellectual organization, that we can see and feel moral distinctions, and that on such an organization sooner or later the moral laws must tell, to such ears must speak, — in this is our hope. For if the prosperity of this country has been merely the obedience of man to the guiding of nature, — of great rivers and prairies, — yet is there fate above fate, if we choose to speak this language; or, if there is fate in corn and cotton, so is there fate in thought, — this, namely, that the largest thought and the widest love are born to victory, and must prevail.

The revolution is the work of no man, but the eternal effervescence of nature. It never did not work. And we say that revolutions beat all the insurgents, be they never so determined and politic; that the great interests of mankind, being at every moment through ages in favor of justice and the largest liberty, will always, from time to time, gain on the adversary and at last win the day. Never country had such a fortune, as men call fortune, as this, in its geography, its history, and in its majestic possibilities.

We have much to learn, much to correct, — a great deal of lying vanity. The spread eagle must fold his foolish wings and be less of a peacock; must keep his wings to carry the thunderbolt when he is commanded. We must realize our rhetoric and our rituals. Our national flag is not affecting, as it should be, because it does not represent the population of the United States, but some Baltimore or Chicago or Cincinnati or Philadelphia caucus; not union or justice, but selfishness and cunning. If we never put on the liberty-cap until we were freemen by love and self-denial, the liberty-cap would mean something. I wish to see America not like the old powers of the earth, grasping, exclusive, and narrow, but a benefactor such as no country ever was, hospitable to all nations, legislating for all nationalities. Nations were made to help each other as much as families were; and all advancement is by ideas, and not by brute force or mechanic force.

In this country, with our practical understanding, there is, at present, a great sensualism, a headlong devotion to trade and to the conquest of the continent, — to each man as large a share of the same as he can carve for himself, — an extravagant confidence in our talent and activity, which becomes, whilst successful, a scornful materialism, — but with the fault, of course, that it has no depth, no reserved force whereon to fall back when a reverse comes.

That repose which is the ornament and ripeness of man is not American. That repose which indicates a faith in the laws of the universe, — a faith that they will fulfil themselves, and are not to be impeded, transgressed, or accelerated. Our people are too slight and vain. They are easily elated and easily depressed. See how fast they extend the fleeting fabric of their trade, — not at all considering the remote reaction and bankruptcy, but with the same abandonment to the moment and the facts of the hour as the Esquimaux who sells his bed in the morning. Our people act on the moment, and from external impulse. They all lean on some other, and this superstitiously, and not from insight of his merit. They follow a fact; they follow success, and not skill. Therefore, as soon as the success stops and the admirable man blunders, they quit him; already they remember that they long ago suspected his judgment, and they transfer the repute of judgment to the next prosperous person who has not yet blundered. Of course this levity makes them as easily despond. It seems as if history gave no account of any society in which despondency came so readily to heart as we see it and feel it in ours. Young men at thirty and even earlier lose all spring and vivacity, and if they fail in their first enterprise throw up the game.

The source of mischief is the extreme difficulty with which men are roused from the torpor of every day. Blessed is all that agitates the mass, breaks up this torpor, and begins motion. *Corpora non agunt nisi soluta;*

the chemical rule is true in mind. Contrast change, interruption, are necessary to new activity and new combinations.

If a temperate wise man should look over our American society, I think the first danger that would excite his alarm would be the European influences on this country.   We buy much of Europe that does not make us better men : and mainly the expensiveness which is ruining that country. ' We import trifles, dancers, singers, laces, books of patterns, modes, gloves, and cologne, manuals of Gothic architecture, steam-made ornaments. America is provincial.   It is an immense Halifax.   See the secondariness and aping of foreign and English life, that runs through this country, in building, in dress, in eating, in books. Every village, every city has its architecture, its costume, its hotel, its private house, its church from England.

Our politics threaten her.   Her manners

threaten us. Life is grown and growing so
costly, that it threatens to kill us. A man
is coming here as there to value himself on
what he can buy. Worst of all, his ex-
pense is not his own, but a far off copy of
Osborne House or the Elysée. The tendency
of this is to make all men alike; to extin-
guish individualism and choke up all the
channels of inspiration from God in man.
We lose our invention and descend into
imitation. · A man no longer conducts his
own life. It is manufactured for him. The
tailor makes your dress; the baker your
bread; the upholsterer — from an imported
book of patterns — your furniture; the Bishop
of London your faith.

In the planters of this country, in the
seventeenth century, the conditions of the
country combined with the impatience of ar-
bitrary power which they brought from England, forced them to a wonderful personal independence and to a certain heroic planting

and trading. Later this strength appeared in the solitudes of the West, where a man is made a hero by the varied emergencies of his lonely farm, and neighborhoods must combine against the Indians, or the horse-thieves, or the river rowdies, by organizing themselves into committees of vigilance. Thus the land and sea educate the people, and bring out presence of mind, self-reliance, and hundred-handed activity. These are the people for an emergency. They are not to be surprised, and can find a way out of any peril. This rough and ready force becomes them, and makes them fit citizens and civilizers. But if we found them clinging to English traditions, which are graceful enough at home, as the English Church, and entailed estates, and distrust of popular election, we should feel this reactionary, and absurdly out of place.

Let the passion for America cast out the passion for Europe. Here let there be what the earth waits for, — exalted manhood.

What this country longs for is personalities, grand persons, to counteract its materialities. For it is the rule of the universe that corn shall serve man, and not man corn.

They who find America insipid,— they for whom London and Paris have spoiled their own homes, can be spared to return to those cities. I not only see a career at home for more genius than we have, but for more than there is in the world.

The class of which I speak make themselves merry without duties. They sit in decorated club-houses in the cities, and burn tobacco and play whist; in the country they sit idle in stores and bar-rooms, and burn tobacco, and gossip and sleep. They complain of the flatness of American life; "America has no illusions, no romance." They have no perception of its destiny. They are not Americans.

The felon is the logical extreme of the epicure and coxcomb. Selfish luxury is the end of both, though in one it is decorated with refinements, and in the other brutal. But my point now is, that this spirit is not American.

Our young men lack idealism. A man for success must not be pure idealist, then he will practically fail ; but he must have ideas, must obey ideas, or he might as well be the horse he rides on. A man does not want to be sun-dazzled, sun-blind; but every man must have glimmer enough to keep him from knocking his head against the walls. And it is in the interest of civilization and good society and friendship, that I dread to hear of well-born, gifted and amiable men, that they have this indifference, disposing them to this despair.

Of no use are the men who study to do exactly as was done before, who can never understand that to-day is a new day. There never was such a combination as this of ours, and the rules to meet it are not set down in any history. We want men of original per-

ception and original action, who can open
their eyes wider than to a nationality, —
namely, to considerations of benefit to the
human race, — can act in the interest of
civilization; men of elastic, men of moral
mind, who can live in the moment and take
a step forward. Columbus was no backward-
creeping crab, nor was Martin Luther, nor
John Adams, nor Patrick Henry, nor Thomas
Jefferson ; and the Genius or Destiny of
America is no log or sluggard, but a man
incessantly advancing, as the shadow on the
dial's face, or the heavenly body by whose
light it is marked.

The flowering of civilization is the finished
man, the man of sense, of grace, of accom-
plishment, of social power, — the gentleman.
What hinders that he be born here ? The
new times need a new man, the complemental
man, whom plainly this country must furnish.
Freer swing his arms ; farther pierce his eyes ;
more forward and forthright his whole build

and rig than the Englishman's, who, we see,
is much imprisoned in his backbone.

'T is certain that our civilization is yet
incomplete, it has not ended, nor given sign
of ending, in a hero. 'T is a wild democracy; the riot of mediocrities and dishones-
ties and fudges. Ours is the age of the om-
nibus, of the third person plural, of Tammany
Hall.

Is it that nature has only so much vital
force, and must dilute it if it is to be mul-
tiplied into millions? The beautiful is never
plentiful. Then Illinois and Indiana, with
their spawning loins, must needs be ordi-
nary.

It is not a question whether we shall be
a multitude of people. No, that has been
conspicuously decided already; but whether
we shall be the new nation, the guide and
lawgiver of all nations, as having clearly
chosen and firmly held the simplest and best
rule of political society.

Now, if the spirit which years ago armed this country against rebellion, and put forth such gigantic energy in the charity of the Sanitary Commission, could be waked to the conserving and creating duty of making the laws just and humane, it were to enroll a great constituency of religious, self-respecting, brave, tender, faithful obeyers of duty, lovers of men, filled with loyalty to each other, and with the simple and sublime purpose of carrying out in private and in public action the desire and need of mankind.

Here is the post where the patriot should plant himself; here the altar where virtuous young men, those to whom friendship is the dearest covenant, should bind each other to loyalty, where genius should kindle its fires and bring forgotten truth to the eyes of men.

Let the good citizen perform the duties put on him here and now. It is not possible to extricate yourself from the questions

in which your age is involved. It is not by
heads reverted to the dying Demosthenes, or
to Luther, or to Wallace, or to George Fox,
or to George Washington, that you can combat the dangers and dragons that beset the
United States at this time. I believe this
cannot be accomplished by dunces or idlers,
but requires docility, sympathy, and religious
receiving from higher principles; for liberty,
like religion, is a short and hasty fruit, and
like all power subsists only by new rallyings
on the source of inspiration. *

Power can be generous. The very grandeur of the means which offer themselves to
us should suggest grandeur in the direction of
our expenditure. If our mechanic arts are
unsurpassed in usefulness, if we have taught
the river to make shoes and nails and carpets,
and the bolt of heaven to write our letters
like a Gillott pen, let these wonders work for
honest humanity, for the poor, for justice,
genius, and the public good. Let us realize

that this country, the last found, is the great charity of God to the human race.

· America should affirm and establish that in no instance shall the guns go in advance of the present right. We shall not make *coups d'état* and afterwards explain and pay, but shall proceed like William Penn, or whatever other Christian or humane person who treats with the Indian or the foreigner, on principles of honest trade and mutual advantage. We can see that the Constitution and the law in America must be written on ethical principles, so that the entire power of the spiritual world shall hold the citizen loyal, and repel the enemy as by force of nature. It should be mankind's bill of rights, or Royal Proclamation of the Intellect ascending the throne, announcing its good pleasure, that now, once for all, the world shall be governed by common sense and law of morals.

The end of all political struggle is to establish morality as the basis of all legislation.

'T is not free institutions, 't is not a democracy that is the end,—no, but only the
means.   Morality is the object of government.   We want a state of things in which
crime will not pay, a state of things which
allows every man the largest liberty compat-
ible with the liberty of every other man.

Humanity asks that government shall not
be ashamed to be tender and paternal, but
that democratic institutions shall be more
thoughtful for the interests of women, for
the training of children, and for the welfare
of sick and unable persons, and serious care
of criminals, than was ever any the best government of the old world.

The genius of the country has marked out
our true policy, — opportunity.   Opportunity
of civil rights, of education, of personal power,
and not less of wealth; doors wide open.   If I
could have it, — free trade with all the world
without toll or custom-houses, invitation as
we now make to every nation, to every race

and skin, white men, red men, yellow men, black men ; hospitality of fair field and equal laws to all. Let them compete, and success to the strongest, the wisest, and the best. The land is wide enough, the soil has bread for all.

I hope America will come to have its pride in being a nation of servants, and not of the served. How can men have any other ambition where the reason has not suffered a disastrous eclipse? Whilst every man can say I serve, — to the whole extent of my being I apply my faculty to the service of mankind in my especial place, — he therein sees and shows a reason for his being in the world, and is not a moth or incumbrance in it.

The distinction and end of a soundly constituted man is his labor. Use is inscribed on all his faculties. Use is the end to which he exists. As the tree exists for its fruit, so a man for his work. A fruitless plant, an idle animal, does not stand in the universe.

They are all toiling, however secretly or slowly, in the province assigned them, and to a use in the economy of the world; the higher and more complex organizations, to higher and more catholic service. And man seems to play, by his instincts and activity, a certain part that even tells on the general face of the planet, drains swamps, leads rivers into dry countries for their irrigation, perforates forests and stony mountain-chains with roads, hinders the inroads of the sea on the continent, as if dressing the globe for happier races.

On the whole, I know that the cosmic results will be the same, whatever the daily events may be. Happily we are under better guidance than of statesmen. Pennsylvania coal mines, and New York shipping, and free labor, though not idealists, gravitate in the ideal direction. Nothing less large than justice can keep them in good temper. Justice satisfies everybody, and justice alone. No monopoly must be foisted in, no weak party or nationality sacrificed, no coward compromise conceded to a strong partner. Every one of these is the seed of vice, war, and national disorganization. It is our part to carry out to the last the ends of liberty and justice. We shall stand, then, for vast interests; north and south, east and west, will be present to our minds, and our vote will be as if they voted, and we shall know that our vote secures the foundations of the state, good-will, liberty and security of traffic and of production, and mutual increase of good-will in the great interests.

 ·Our helm is given up to a better guidance than our own; the course of events is quite too strong for any helmsman, and our little wherry is taken in tow by the ship of the great Admiral which knows the way, and has the force to draw men and states and planets to their good.

Such and so potent is this high method by

which the Divine Providence sends the chief-
est benefits under the mask of calamities, that
I do not think we shall by any perverse in-
genuity prevent the blessing.

In seeing this guidance of events, in seeing
this felicity without example that has rested
on the Union thus far, I find new confidence
for the future. I could heartily wish that our
will and endeavor were more active parties
to the work. But I see in all directions the
light breaking. Trade and government will
not alone be the favored aims of mankind,
but every useful, every elegant art, every
exercise of imagination, the height of reason,
the noblest affection, the purest religion will
find their home in our institutions, and write
our laws for the benefit of men.

www.ingramcontent.com/pod-product-compliance
Lightning Source LLC
Chambersburg PA
CBHW021557270326
41931CB00009B/1257